D1603597

these words are
FOR YOU

Written by M.H. Clark
Illustrated by Jill Labieniec

If you're holding this book, then these words are for you. They've come a long way to find you, to sit with you. To be with you now.

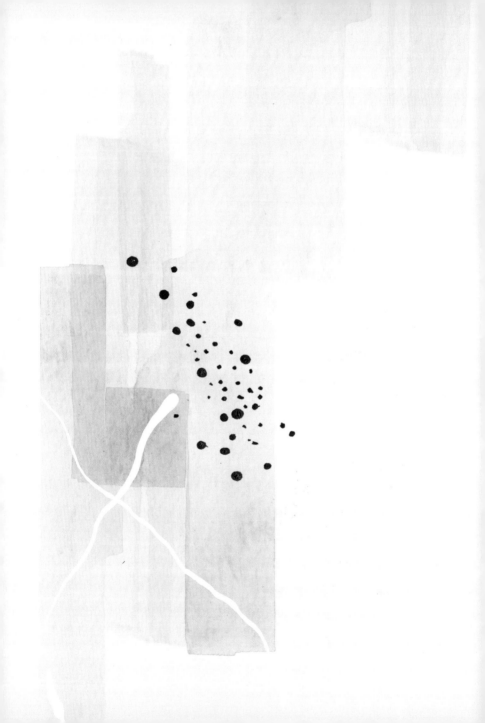

These words are small, but they breathe as you breathe. They shine their own light in the dark.

And they don't change what is happening,
but they're here as it happens.

They are with you in this moment.

They are with you if the moment
feels slow, or if it feels stuck.
If it feels hopeless, or anxious, or lost.

*These words, at this moment,
call you back to yourself. They call you
back to whatever deep emotion is
weighing on your heart.*

Because the places you are hurting
are also filled with life.

And the tenderness in you
is part of your gift.

And all the ways that you
are human—complex and deep
and true—are the ways that the
world connects to you.

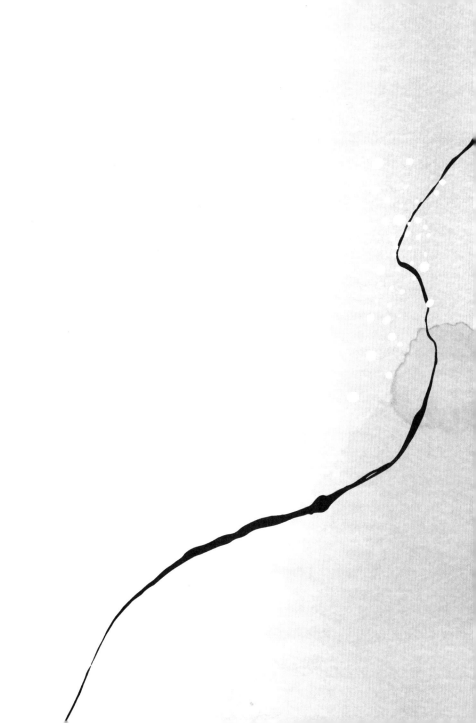

These words are here today,
with what is true today.

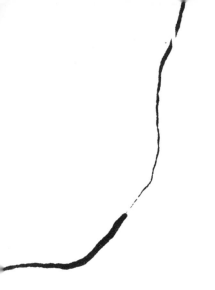

And what is true today is shifting,

ever so slightly.

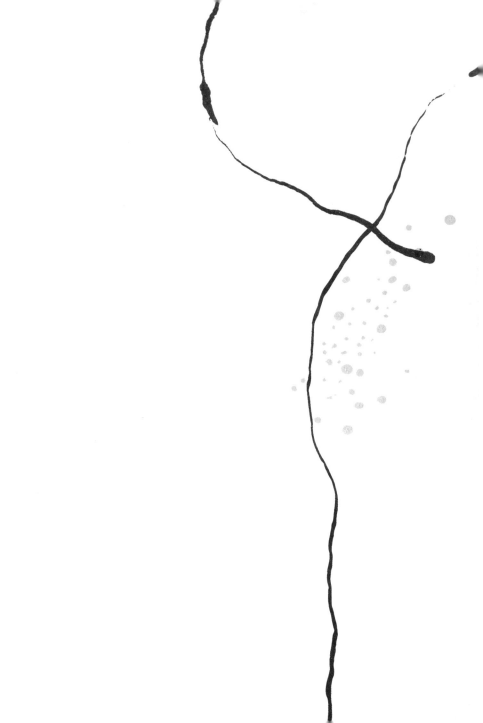

It is changing, ever so slightly.

*And the future leans back to you now
and says, keep going.*

And the future leans back to you now
and says, you do not need to triumph.
You do not need to be any stronger
than you are.

*You do not need to move through this
more quickly than you're able.*

You only have to be right here
and hold your heart with care.

Hold your vulnerability with care.
Hold your complexity, your hurt.

Hold your hope for something more.

Hold the feeling that is present now.
And know that you are not stuck.

You are moving, even now.
Even now, you are transforming.

You are taking this feeling and evolving it.

You are shaping this feeling into part of what has been.

You are letting the wave of it move through you.

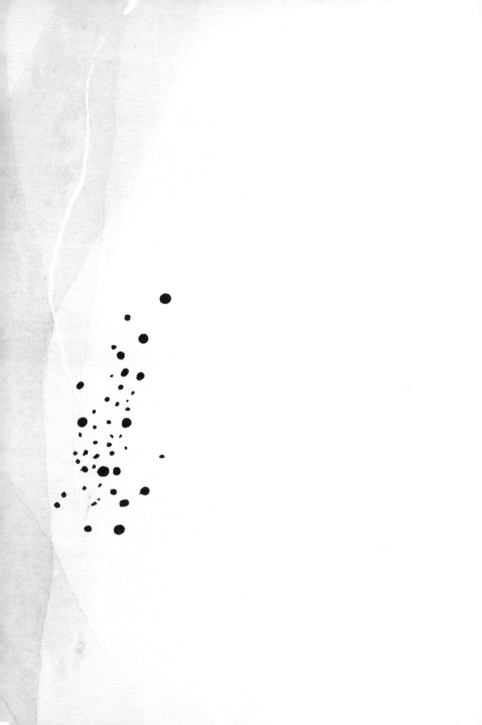

These words are for you,
as this wave opens into another.
And into another, still.

These words are here for the process,

as long as it takes.

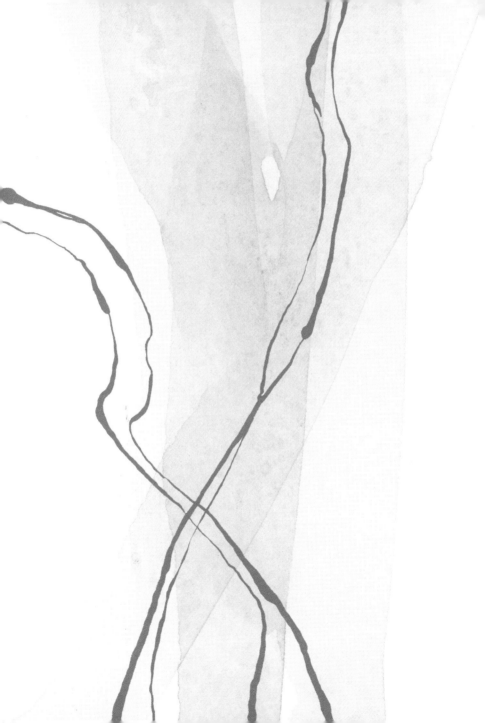

They are here for all the subtle shifts inside.

And when the time is right,
they will be with you
as you let what's next arrive.

COMPENDIUM.
live inspired

With special thanks to the entire
Compendium family.

Credits:

Written by: M.H. Clark

Edited by: Ruth Austin

Illustrated by: Jill Labieniec

Library of Congress Control Number: 2018955814
ISBN: 978-1-946873-61-3

1st printing. Printed in China with soy inks.